monday morning®

TEACHER TIPS FOR
Circle Time

by Dana McMillan and the Learning Exchange, Inc.
Illustrated by Corbin Hillam

Publisher: Roberta Suid
Editor: Carol Whiteley
Production: Susan Pinkerton
Cover: David Hale

monday
morning.

Monday Morning is a registered trademark of
Monday Morning Books, Inc.

ISBN 1-878279-08-4

Printed in the United States of America

9 8 7 6 5 4

CONTENTS

INTRODUCTION

The activities in *Teacher Tips for Circle Time* were developed for those times in the early childhood classroom when you want to work with all the children as they sit in a circle on the floor. Circle activities need special consideration and design: They must keep all the children actively involved and interested, but they should also reinforce the skills you have chosen to work on.

The ideas that grew into *Teacher Tips for Circle Time* were developed and used by a group of early childhood teachers who work with children ranging from three to seven years of age. The activities were classroom-tested—and enjoyed—before they were compiled into this book. The songs are all original, created by our group to promote children's particular skills or interests. We coupled our new words to familiar songs with repetitive elements, making it easier for both you and your children to work with them.

The activities in *Teacher Tips for Circle Time* are organized into skill areas by chapter:

Listening
Small- and Large-Motor Skills
Discrimination
Problem Solving
Patterning
Music

There is no particular order to the chapters, but some of them contain activities that are more suitable for younger children. As with all resource materials, you, the teacher, must select the activities and materials that are appropriate for your class.

Each chapter in the book contains a special "One-on-One" page. The activities on this page are for parents who want to work at home with their child in fun, interactive ways. Many of the activities described on the "One-on-One" pages are variations of those you will be doing at school. These home versions will give the children further opportunities to continue learning and developing skills when they are outside the classroom. The One-on-One activities are also particularly appropriate for specialists who work with special education students in one-on-one situations.

Most of the activities require no materials. Some use very standard items you already have in your classroom, and a few require things the children have with them, such as their shoes. If an activity does ask you to collect certain items, it will be quick and easy to do. Try to look over each activity before you begin so you can collect any needed materials ahead of time.

Working with and sharing ideas with outstanding professionals was, for me, a wonderful part of creating this book. I hope that the activities *Teacher Tips for Circle Time* contains bring new fun and learning to those times when you, your class, and their families want to work together in productive ways.

Dana McMillan
The Learning Exchange, Inc.
2720 Walnut
Kansas City, Missouri 64108

The Learning Exchange is a not-for-profit educational resource center. Its staff members and consultants are dedicated to the goal of improving the quality of education by working with teachers to improve the quality of instruction. The Learning Exchange establishes partnerships with the business and educational communities to achieve this goal.

IN APPRECIATION
The Learning Exchange gratefully acknowledges the following educators for the ideas they contributed to this book:
    Christy Buckner
    Kathy Feldmiller
    Jean Kozak
    Dottie Lowe
    Linda Steimer

CHAPTER 1

LISTENING

Listening activities are important because:
• The ability to listen is a key skill needed for all other learning.
• Listening awareness will promote audio discrimination.
• Language skills are developed when children are encouraged to listen.

To promote success in listening activities:
• Help the children find a comfortable listening position. You might want to have them sit on the floor with their legs folded and their hands in their lap. Or you might have them try the pike position—resting on the knees with the legs folded underneath.
• Use a simple song to signal to the children that it is time to come to the circle for a listening activity. "The Listening Song" and "Everybody, Sit Down" in this chapter work well.
• Be sure the activities you use are designed to be fun.
• Define a space for each child to sit in in the circle. You can do this by marking the floor with tape, using carpet squares, or cutting and laminating construction paper letters, numbers, shapes, or colors to tape onto the floor.
• Sit on a low chair in the circle; try not to be separate from the children or standing above them. Use a quiet voice and try to limit distractions in the room. Most important, make eye contact with the children. Reinforce the children's listening by demonstrating that you are listening to them.
• Plan your listening activities for the most effective times during the day: first thing in the morning, at short transition times throughout the day, and at the end of the day before the children leave.

Word for the Day

Make a simple mask from a piece of lightweight fabric by folding the fabric in half and stapling the two sides. Use a permanent marker to draw nonfrightening features on the mask; add yarn hair if you wish. Have a child who'd like to wear the mask slip it over his or her head. Then whisper a word for the day to the child: "The word for the day is 'whiskers.' " Ask the other children to listen while the child who is wearing the mask says the word for the day. Younger children will forget who is under the mask and will need to use their listening skills to guess who is speaking. Have the masked child continue to say the word for the day until someone guesses who he or she is. If necessary, give clues about the speaker, for example, "Our speaker is wearing a red ribbon on her ponytail."

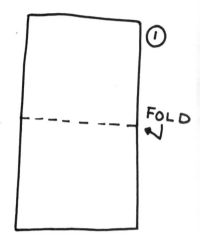

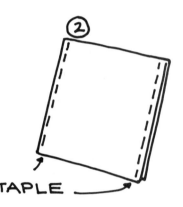

Variation: When playing the game with older children, take one child out of the room while the others are busy. Tell the child the word for the day and help him or her put on the mask. When the other children have gathered in the circle, have the masked child come into the room and say the word for the day. Allow the children to use their listening skills and guess who is under the mask.

The Listening Song

Use this song to help the children prepare for a listening activity or to signal the transition from an activity to listening time.

    Open, shut them, open, shut them, let your hands go clap.

    Open, shut them, open, shut them, lay them in your lap.

8

Who's That Knocking on My Door?

Have the children sit on the floor in a circle. Place one chair facing out of the circle and choose one child to sit in it. Choose another child to go behind the chair and knock on the back. Have the child in the chair say, "Who's that knocking on my door?" The child who is knocking should say, "Let me come in." Then ask the child in the chair to try to guess who is speaking. If the child guesses correctly, pick another child to knock. If the child who knocked is not named, he or she takes the position in the chair.

Variation: Older children may use various voice disguises to try to stump the child in the chair. You may also have "twins" come calling by choosing two children to knock on the door and speak at the same time. The child in the chair must name both children to stay in the chair.

Everybody, Sit Down

Use this song to call the children together for a listening activity.

Everybody, sit down, sit down, sit down.
Everybody, sit down, just like (say the name of a child who is sitting in the circle).

Variations:

Everybody, stand up...
Everybody, wash hands...
Everybody, stretch up...

I See

Describe a general personal characteristic and ask all the children who have that characteristic to stand up. For example, say, "If you have hair on your head, stand up." Narrow down the characteristic and ask those children who have the new characteristic to sit down. For example, after all the children with hair are standing, ask the children with brown hair to sit down. Then ask children with ponytails to sit, then children with barrettes in their hair, and so on until no one is left standing.

Variations: Describe two characteristics when you work with older children. For example, after everyone with hair is standing, you could ask all children with blonde hair in two ponytails to sit down. Also consider using characteristics that relate to birthdays, letters in the children's names, clothes, or shoes.

New Shoes

When children arrive at class with new shoes or new clothes they are excited about, use this activity to announce the important new item at circle time. When everyone is seated in the circle, say, in a sing-song voice:

New shoes, new shoes (or whatever the new item is),
(The child's name) has new shoes.

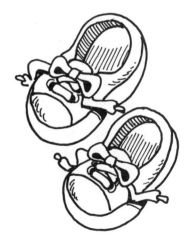

Then ask the child to walk around the circle and show the new apparel to the other children. The child may also want to tell something about the place where the item was purchased, how it was chosen, or the occasion it was purchased for.

The Rhyming Game

While the children are in the circle, say the following verses in a sing-song way. Leave off the last word of each line and let the children make the rhyme.

   I am a bee and I climb a (tree).
   I am a bear and I sit in a (chair).
   I am a rat and I wear a (hat).
   I am a mouse and I live in a (house).
   I am a chick and I feel real (sick).
   I am a pig and I dance a (jig).
   I am a duck and I have good (luck).

Variation: Help older children make a list of all the animals, foods, or types of transportation they can think of and write the list on a large chart pad. Read each item on the list and have the children pick a word to rhyme with each one. In a list of foods, for example, "bread" could rhyme with "head." Write down the rhyming words and then say the pairs, one at a time. Encourage the children to make up a nonsense rhyme for each of the pairs. For example, "If I had some bread, it would be on my head."

The Rhyming Book

Choose a storybook that is written in rhyme to read to the children. Tell them that you are going to read the book to them two times. The first time they should listen to the story carefully because the second time they are going to help you read it. Read the story through once, emphasizing the rhyme combinations. On the second reading, stop before completing a rhyme and allow the children to say the rhyming word.

Albert, the Puppet

Purchase a puppet or create your own using simple materials found in your home or school. Choose a name for the puppet that the children will enjoy—perhaps Albert. Use Albert (or the name you choose) to give directions to the children. For example, you might say, "Boys and girls, Albert has something to say to us. What is it, Albert?" Put the puppet to your ear as if it is talking to you. Then say, "Albert says it's time for us to get ready to go outside. Oh, wait, he wants to tell me something else. What is it, Albert?" Then have Albert "tell" you any specific directions you want to give to the children. Relay Albert's message: "Albert says to remind you that you should zip up your coats and put on mittens and hats. He doesn't want you to be chilly outside."

Variations: Albert can give directions for various activities. He can also be used to visit learning areas in the classroom and encourage the children while they are working or playing. Use Albert to introduce a guest, a new child, or a parent.

Directions, Please

Seated in the circle, explain the rules of this game. Tell the children that, beginning with you, each person must give the person on his or her left something to do. The job or action must be something that can be done while sitting in the circle, for example, putting your legs out straight or counting to three. When the job is done, the child who did it gives new directions to the child on the left, and so on around the circle.

Variation: Older children can extend the game by giving two or three directions: "Put your hands on your head and then touch your toes."

To Our Work Now We Must Go

Use this simple song to dismiss the children from the circle to go to different learning areas. The song will encourage the children to listen for their name.

To our work now we must go,
Learning names row by row.
Say it loud and say it clear,
Say your name so we can hear.

After singing the song through once, dismiss a small group of children to a certain area of the room. Say, for example, "Shelly, Cara, Bobby. You may go to the block area." Then sing the song again and name another group of children to go to a different area.

Variations: You may also use the song to dismiss several children to another activity while the others remain in the circle and continue an activity. The song is also handy to dismiss small groups to get ready for lunch or nap time or to prepare for leaving for the day.

The Sharing Hat

Add a new twist to your sharing time—and help children be better listeners—by creating a funny hat for the child who is sharing to wear. Use an old hat and add odds and ends of yarn, lace, netting, and/or felt. You might glue on shapes cut from the felt or add buttons and cut button holes to allow the children to create their own look. Hold the hat in your lap at sharing time and then choose the first child to begin sharing by passing the hat to him or her. The child can wear the hat while sharing and then pass it to the next child.

Hi, What's Your News?

As the children gather for circle time at the beginning of the day, take the roll but do it by calling out each child's name and then asking if he or she has anything to share since the last time you were together. For example, say, "Missy, good morning. Do you have any news to share?" Have a chart pad and marker ready when you work with older children. After one child shares something, call on another child and ask him or her what you should write on the chart about the child who just spoke. For example, after Missy has shared her news with the group, call on Tony and say, "What do you think I should put on the chart to remind us about Missy's news?" Display the chart paper on an easel.

Who's That Talking?

While the children are working independently at learning areas, use a tape recorder and microphone to record each of their voices. Later, at circle time, play the recording for the children. Stop the tape after each child speaks and ask, "Who do you think that is?" Allow the children to guess. Younger children may not recognize their own voice or remember what they said on the tape. Play the entire tape, encouraging the children to listen carefully and try to guess each child who is speaking.

Variation: Make a tape of parents, familiar school personnel, or TV personalities and allow the children to guess who is speaking.

Old MacDonald Had a Farm

Sing "Old MacDonald Had a Farm." Stop after the line "And on his farm he had some . . . ." Choose one child to name an animal. Print the animal selected on chart paper. Then repeat the song line and include the animal that the child named. Finish the song and then begin again, following the same procedure. This time, however, the child you call on must name the first animal and add a new one. Continue to record each animal named and point to the appropriate name as the line is sung. Continue until the children cannot think of any more animals.

Variation: Collect pictures of animals. As a child names an animal to add to the song, allow him or her to hold its picture. As the song continues, have each child with the appropriate picture hold it up as the animal is named.

One-on-One: Parent-Child Listening Activities

WHO'S THAT TALKING?

With your child, watch a familiar television show with characters he or she knows well. After a few minutes, ask your child to listen carefully with eyes closed. When a character comes on the show, ask who is speaking. Allow your child to open his or her eyes and see if the answer is correct. Take turns playing the game during the show.

WHO'S THAT KNOCKING ON MY DOOR?

Collect a number of your child's favorite dolls and toys. Then seat your child in a chair that is turned away from the collection. Pick up one of the dolls or toys and then knock on the back of the chair. Help your child form a question to ask who is knocking on the "door." Disguise your voice for the toy to give a clue. For example, you might say, "It's me, your favorite bedtime friend." Provide more clues if your child needs help determining which doll or toy is knocking.

THE RHYMING GAME

Ask your child to choose two rhyming words and make a nonsense sentence from them. For example, your child might choose "bear" and "hair" and say, "If I had a bear, I'd lose my hair." Let your child make several nonsense rhymes.

RHYMING BOOKS

When you read a book with rhymes to your child, leave out the last word in a rhyming sentence and ask your child what word he or she thinks would finish the sentence. Encourage your child to think of a word that rhymes. Then read the complete original sentence to see how the author finished the rhyme.

FOLLOWING DIRECTIONS

Make a game out of following directions by asking your child to do one fun thing, perhaps hopping on one foot. Then add a second direction, for example, hop on one foot and touch your nose. Encourage your child to listen to both directions before doing them. When he or she is successful with two-step directions, you may want to add a third.

CHAPTER 2

LARGE- AND SMALL-MOTOR SKILLS

Large- and small-motor activities are important because:
• Small-motor development increases children's ability to hold utensils, writing tools, and scissors. Without the development of small-motor muscles, children will be frustrated doing these types of tasks and should not be expected to do them.
• Though large-motor development is often associated with out-door play, large-motor activities during circle time can also release energy.
• They allow children to use their motor skills in a fun, non-frustrating way.

To promote success in large- and small-motor activities:
• Do not expect all the children to be able to do the activities in the same way or with the same amount of success. For some children, coloring with crayons is frustrating but using Goop (a mixture of glue and white starch) is fun.
• Be sure the children work on small-motor activities when they are not tired or easily distracted. Watch for signs of frustration and allow the children to move on to another activity when they need something else to do. Try alternating the activities in this chapter with others in the book.
• Let the large-motor circle activities be a fun break from quiet circle activities; they can provide the children with exercise when play periods are not scheduled.
• Let the children enjoy some of the small-motor activities while seated in a circle; young children do not have to be seated at a table to have success with small-motor projects.
• Monitor the work children do with materials such as scissors. Talk with the children about why they should not put small objects in their mouths, run with sharp objects in their hands, or swing objects near other children.

Clay Press

Gather a garlic press, some clay, a plastic bowl, and waxed paper. Demonstrate to the children how to put a small amount of clay into the garlic press and squeeze it to make long clay strings; the squeezing motion will strengthen the muscles in the hands and fingers. Provide each pair of children with a small amount of clay on a piece of waxed paper. Give one pair of children the garlic press and allow the other pairs to play with their clay. Have the first pair press out clay strings, put them into the bowl, and pass the press to the next pair of students. The clay strings may be used as play food in the housekeeping area (be sure the children know not to eat it) or it may be glued onto lightweight cardboard in a texture design.

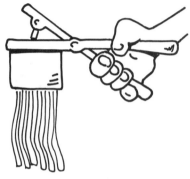

Let Your Fingers Do the Walking

Draw a simple path on a piece of construction paper. Print "Start" on one end and "Finish" on the other. Place the path in the center of the circle and demonstrate to the children how to use their first two fingers to walk on the path from start to finish. Choose one child to "walk" along the path. Then have the other children take turns. Children who are competent at coordinating the movement of their two fingers can use them to walk backwards or to "kick" through the path. Older children can walk on a path made from toothpicks, paper clips, sugar cubes, or small blocks.

Variations: Mix a small amount of bright tempera paint that will show up well on construction paper. Give each of the children a large sheet of construction paper. Then let them create their own finger paths or mazes by placing the tips of their two walking fingers in the tempera paint and drawing on their paper.

Clothespin Drop

This activity will increase eye-hand coordination. Begin by giving a non-spring-type clothespin and a plastic milk container with the lid off to one child in the circle. Have the child put the milk container on the floor and stand above it. Then have the child try to drop the clothespin into the milk container. Let the child practice a few times and then give him or her four more clothespins. See how many of the five pins the child can drop into the container. Reinforce the number by saying, for example, "You put two of the five clothespins into the container."

Variation: Extend the activity by having older children graph the clothespin drop results. Have them list all the children's names across the top of a sheet of poster board. Then have them put a peel-off dot below each child's name for each clothespin he or she was able to drop into the container.

Mary	Meg	Troy	T.J.
•	•	•	•
•	•		•
	•		•
	•		•
			•

Goop

In a plastic bowl with a lid that forms a tight seal, mix equal amounts of white glue and liquid starch—Goop. When the children are seated in the circle, provide each one with a plastic place mat or a sheet of waxed paper. Put a small amount of Goop on each mat. Encourage the children to pull and stretch their Goop, increasing the strength of the small muscles in their hands. Store the Goop in the plastic bowl with the lid sealed.

Face Play

To encourage the children to use the muscles in their face, help them decide how to make their faces impersonate taffy or play-dough, a sponge that is soaking up water, and oatmeal cookie dough. Encourage them to look at each other's faces while they experiment. Pass a mirror around the circle for the children to see their own faces.

Variations: Ask older children to "save their faces" by making a mask of their play face from art materials. The mask could be displayed on a bulletin board with a description the child dictates, for example, "My face is like a sponge all filled up with water."

Who's Leading the Circle?

Choose one child to leave the room. Pick another child to be the leader. Have the leader think of several movements for all the children in the circle to follow. Then ask the child who left the room to return and try to guess who is leading the children in the movements. Encourage the child who is leading to change movements. Allow the child who is guessing three chances to discover the leader. If the leader is identified, the guesser may choose the next child to leave the room. If the leader is not identified, he or she leaves the room while you choose a new leader.

Lids and Jars

Collect a number of clean, empty jars and lids of various sizes: baby food jars, small bottles for olives or cherries, salad dressing bottles, peanut butter jars, and so on. Take the lids off and place both the jars and the lids in a large box. At circle time, pass the box around the circle and ask each child to choose a jar and a lid. Encourage the children to try to match a jar to its correct lid, but allow them to use their problem-solving skills to decide which lid fits the jar. Ask the children to put each lid on so that if the jar were filled with water nothing would leak out; the twisting motion will help develop the small muscles in the hands and fingers. Have the children exchange jars when necessary and continue to match jars with lids.

Stringing Pasta

To help the children develop the small-muscle coordination needed to thread a needle, collect large tube-shaped pasta shells, one-foot lengths of yarn, scissors, and a plastic margarine tub lid for each child. Cut a hole in the center of each lid and put a length of yarn through each, knotting the yarn beneath the hole. If you're working with younger children or children with poor eye-hand coordination, you may also want to dip the free end of each yarn length into white glue and let it dry overnight. This will give the yarn a firm threading end. At the circle, provide each child with several pieces of pasta and a lid with attached yarn. Demonstrate how to string the pasta onto the yarn by laying the lid on the floor, holding the yarn up with one hand, and stringing the pasta onto the yarn with the other hand. Then have the children string their pasta.

Variations: Provide several types of pasta for the children to alternate on their yarn. The pasta may be colored with food coloring (see "Macaroni Necklaces" in Chapter 5).

Pinching a Bubble

Use packing material with small air bubbles to help develop the children's small-muscle strength. Cut a small square of the material for each child. At the circle, give the children their squares and demonstrate how to pop the bubbles by using a forefinger and the thumb to squeeze out the air. Allow the children to pop as many bubbles as they can. Children who have difficulty using their finger and thumb may need help holding their square or help pressing their finger and thumb together.

Riding a Bike

Sit the children in the circle and then ask them to lay back with their legs in the air. Tell them they are going on a bike ride. Demonstrate how they can move their legs in a circular motion as if they were pedaling a bike. Encourage the children to go slowly at first and then to increase their speed. If convenient, play music that has various tempos. Help the children match the pace of their leg movements to the music.

Wiggle Toes

Allow the children to remove their shoes and socks. Then have them sit in a circle with their feet pointed toward the center. Give various commands to encourage the children to move and control their feet and toes: toes in, toes out, toes up, toes down, and wiggle toes. As the children follow your directions, say this poem:

Our toes go in, our toes go out,
And when they do we laugh a lot.
Our toes go up, our toes go down,
And mostly they just wiggle about.

Clowning Around

Help the children all face in the same direction in the circle. Tell them that on your command you want them to walk around the circle and follow these directions:

Clowns walk with their toes pointing in.
Clowns walk with their toes pointing out.
Clowns walk slowly.
Clowns walk quickly.
Clowns walk way down low to the ground.
Clowns walk way up high.

If possible, play a recording of circus music to set the pace.

Frisbee Passing

Bring a Frisbee to the circle for a game that allows the children to use their large muscles but remain in the circle. Start the game by passing the Frisbee to the child next to you, and have it pass all around the circle. When the Frisbee returns to you, explain that you are now going to pass it around the circle in a new way. Use one of the following methods each time the Frisbee reaches you; call out the command so everyone knows it:

Pass the Frisbee over your head.
Pass the Frisbee with your hands crossed.
Pass the Frisbee under your leg.
Pass the Frisbee behind your back.

Variation: For older children, choose a child to lead the Frisbee passing. Stipulate that once a passing method has been used, it can't be used again.

Circle Musical Chairs

Play a new version of Musical Chairs using cloth place mats or squares of fabric cut to place mat size. Space the mats around the circle and ask each child to stand behind a mat as you explain the rules of the game. To begin, put on a record or cassette and have the children walk in a circle behind the place mats while the music plays. When the music stops, the children should sit on the place mat closest to them. When the children stand, remove one place mat and start the music again. Have the children walk around the circle until you stop the music once more. Encourage the children to find a place mat to sit on. The child who ends up without a place mat should go and sit in the center of the circle. Continue removing one place mat and sending one child to the center after each round until only one child is left. That child is the winner of the game.

Hit the Bucket

Collect as many beanbags as there are children. Distribute the beanbags and place a plastic bucket or tub in the center of the circle. Tell the children to aim at the bucket and try to toss their beanbag into it. When everyone has thrown a beanbag, collect them and have the children try again. Let the class continue while you observe which children consistently hit the target and which need more practice. Some children who seem less able to hit the target may need to move closer.

Run, Little Bear

Use a stuffed bear to play this circle game. Seat the children on chairs in a circle. Then ask them to pass the bear around the circle as you play some music. Without notice, stop the music and say, "Run, little bear." Have the child who is holding the bear just then stand up and run around the outside of the circle. When the child reaches his or her original seat, start the music again and have the child begin passing the bear.

Silent Motions

Make a set of cards like the ones in the illustration; use 5" by 7" pieces of card stock. At the circle, choose one child to be the leader of the game. Allow the leader to choose a card and show it to the children without saying anything. Then ask the children to match their bodies to the way the figure in the card is standing. Have the leader decide if the children match the example and help anyone who does not match it. Let the leader choose another child to become the leader, and let that child choose a new card.

One-on-One: Parent-Child Large- and Small-Motor Skills Activities

1. To strengthen the muscles in your child's hands, allow him or her to use a garlic press with washable playdough or clay. Cover a work area with waxed paper. Then let your child squeeze the playdough or clay through the press to create long, thin strips that are fun to play with.

2. Ice tongs or a similar pinching tool can also develop the hand muscles. Provide your child with such a tool plus a container of cotton balls and an empty container. Demonstrate how to use the tongs to move one cotton ball at a time to the empty bowl.

3. To increase your child's eye-hand coordination, play a game with non-spring-type clothespins and an empty plastic milk container. Put the container, with the lid off, on the floor; have your child stand above it. Then ask your child to drop the clothespins into the milk container opening. Allow plenty of time for practice.

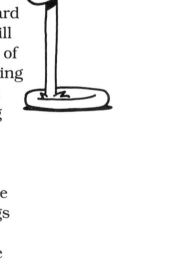

4. Put on some fun music and encourage your child to use large muscle groups while exercising. Some exercises you may want to ask your child to do are: lay on your back and move your legs like you're riding a bike; stretch your arms up and out; touch your toes; lay on the floor and push your tummy up; and lift your shoulders.

5. Make a safe balance beam by placing a length of sturdy board between two bricks. Place the balance beam in an area that will allow your child to feel comfortable walking on it, without fear of being hit by or falling on something. Assist your child in crossing the beam until he or she feels comfortable going alone. When your child is able to cross the beam easily, assist with walking backward on it.

6. Ring toss activities are great for developing eye-hand coordination and for using large muscles. Place a dowel stick in the ground, with a foot of dowel above ground. Use rubber jar rings or make cardboard rings to toss. Allow your child to stand as close as necessary to be successful, and encourage tossing the rings over the dowel. When your child seems ready, challenge him or her to move back a step and try hitting the target from the new spot. Make the game challenging by counting the number of "ringers" out of five tries from each new distance.

CHAPTER 3

DISCRIMINATION

Discrimination activities are important because:
• The ability to discriminate differences is a key concept needed for math.
• Discovering differences and becoming able to verbalize those differences extends the young child's development.
• When young children are encouraged to find differences, they are developing critical thinking and organizational thinking skills.

To promote success in discrimination activities:
• Watch for opportunities during circle time discussions to lead the children to look for things that are alike or different.
• Provide as many opportunities as possible for the children to give their opinion on a subject. One way to encourage more verbal answers is to avoid asking questions that require only a yes or no response. Circle time creates good opportunities for asking questions that encourage greater responses.
• Find unplanned-for opportunities to expand your curriculum by observing the children in work or play areas and guiding them to make observations. A child playing in the sandbox can explain how sand feels different from water.
• Accustom the children to being asked, "How is this different from that?" This will develop more fluency in their thinking and help expand their ideas more easily.
• Encourage the children at every opportunity possible to explain how things are alike and how they are different in the classroom. When encouraged, children will point out how the tables in the art center are different from those in the dramatic play center, and so on. These informal discussions will help you reach your goal of promoting discrimination skills.

What's Missing?

Choose a topic, for example, Halloween, and ask the children to think of as many things as they can that remind them of Halloween, such as witches, brooms, and jack-o'-lanterns. As each item is suggested, make a simple representational drawing on the chalkboard. When all the items have been drawn, ask the children to cover their eyes. Then erase one of the objects from the board. When the children uncover their eyes, ask them to determine which drawing is missing from the board.

Variations: Collect a tray of small items, such as toy cars and animals, paper clips, and pennies. Let the children study it. Put up a screen between the children and the tray and then remove one of the items. Remove the screen. Tell the children to guess what is missing from the tray. Use different colors of construction paper cutouts for older children.

What Doesn't Belong?

Make a collection of small items that would be associated as a set, for example, plastic farm animals, toy cars, toy trucks, plastic fruit, crayons, or rocks. Place one set of items, plus one item that should not be in the set, on a tray. Pass the tray around the circle and ask the children to look at the set but not say anything. When the tray has been passed to each child, have everyone tell you, all together, which item doesn't belong.

Variation: Let older children make more difficult determinations: between one zoo animal and a set of farm animals, a piece of fruit and a set of vegetables, or one green item with a set of blue items that are like the green item except for color.

Class Collections

Send a note home to parents asking for their help in establishing class collections. Appropriate collection items might be keys, bottle caps, seashells, rocks, golf tees, buttons, and nuts and bolts. Place each collection in a small box and label the outside of the box with a picture of the item and the word name. Store the collections where the children can easily reach them and encourage the children to use the collection boxes during free choice times (the boxes may also be used with other activities in this and other chapters in the book). During circle time, pass several collection boxes around. Ask each child to choose any two items from one box. For example, one child may choose two keys, another two seashells. Encourage the children to find something that makes the two items different from each other and share the difference with the group.

Treasure Walk

Allow the children to each decorate a paper bag to take on a walk outside. Tell the children they may each bring back three things from the walk as long as the items fit in the bag and are different from each other. At circle time, ask each child to show the three things from his or her bag. Encourage the children to discuss their choices and how the items they found are alike and different. Have the children determine if they have items that can be added to the collection boxes used in the previous activity. If they do, ask them which boxes the items should go in and why.

Variation: Let older children keep their bag contents a surprise. Then, in the circle, let each child in turn describe one of the objects in his or her bag. The child who guesses the item correctly may describe the next item.

Unit Blocks

Bring unit blocks of various shapes, sizes, and colors to the circle and lay them on the floor in the center. Hold up one block for all the children to see and then ask one child to find a block that is larger. When she or he has found a larger block, ask the other children, "How did Tiffany know that the block was larger?" Encourage the children to verbalize the ways that they discriminate among the sizes of blocks. Then continue working with the blocks, asking the children to find a smaller block, one of a different color, and one that is about the same size as your block but shaped differently.

Variation: When older children work with the unit blocks, hand one block to each child. Hold up your block and ask each child to describe one thing that is different about his or her block and yours, and one thing that is the same.

Marker Tops

Use the tops of markers for a discrimination activity involving colors. Provide each child with a small bowl or margarine tub and a collection of marker tops. Instruct the children to sort the markers into colors and each choose one color to place in a bowl. Ask each child to tell the others in the circle which color he or she chose. If some children choose the same color, encourage them to combine their bowls. Add some additional markers and allow the children to work individually to sort the marker tops into the appropriate bowls.

Soft and Loud Sounds

Make a soft/loud spinner like the one in the illustration by cutting a circle from poster board or oak tag; add a drawing and attach an arrow with a brad. Pass the spinner to one of the children seated in the circle and have him or her spin the arrow. If it points to the "Soft" side, ask the child to make a soft sound. If it points to the "Loud" side, ask the child to make a loud sound. Pass the spinner to another child and follow the same procedure, but ask the second child to make a sound that is softer or louder than the one the first child made. Continue until no one can make a softer or louder sound.

Variation: Allow each child who spins to choose an object in the classroom to make the necessary sound. Encourage the children to think of as many things as possible that could make a noise. Once an object has been used, it may not be chosen again.

Before and After

To help children understand the concept of before and after and discriminate between the two, collect pictures of a chick, a bowl of pudding or jello, toast, and an ice cube. While the children are seated in the circle, show them one of the pictures and ask, "What do you think happened before this picture?" Encourage the children to tell a story if they need to. Then ask, "What do you think will happen after this picture?"

Variation: Use pictures of children looking happy, sad, or scared. Ask the same questions as above, and encourage the children to describe events that would make the people in the pictures feel as they do.

Numbers

Make a chart like the one in the illustration by gluing library pockets in rows on a piece of poster board. Use a marker to print a number from 1 to 10 on each of the pockets. Then put stickers on index cards to make number cards, putting one sticker on one card, two on another, and so on up to 10. Make duplicates so that each child in the class gets a card. At circle time, put the cards in a basket and pass the basket around the circle so that each child may choose a card. Mount the poster on an easel so the children can reach the pockets. When all the children have a card, ask them to look at the chart and be ready to tell which pocket their card goes in. Allow each child to come to the chart and place his or her card in the pocket.

Variations: Place the chart and cards in a learning area for independent work. Have older children use numbers up to 20, upper- and lower-case letters, or beginning sounds and pictures.

Partners

Before the children sit down at circle time, ask them to find a partner to sit with. Go around the circle and ask each pair to show themselves to the group by standing up. Reinforce the partners by saying, "Jennifer and Luke are partners." Then ask each pair to think of a way that they are alike, and share it with the rest of the class. For example, the partners may both be girls, both have brown hair, both have shoes that tie, or both have a baby in the family. If one set of partners has a difficult time thinking of how the two are alike, ask the rest of the group to help them find a similarity. When every pair has found a likeness, ask the children to switch partners and find differences, using the same method.

What's My Group?

Choose three children to stand in the center of the circle. Ask the rest of the children to look at the group carefully and then ask them what is alike about the three children. Encourage as many answers as possible, for example, hair color, clothes, shoes. Allow each of the three children to choose another child to take his or her place. Then play the game again.

Making Sets

Gather the following items and bring them to the circle: a piece of paper, a pencil, a bottle, a lid, a bowl, and a cup. Place the items in the center of the circle and ask the children to name what they see. Then choose one child to show two items that go together, such as the paper and the pencil. Continue asking children for items that go together, moving beyond the obvious answers to expand the children's thinking. After each set is proposed, ask the child, "Why do you think those two things go together?"

Variation: Choose six children to each find something in the room to bring to the circle. Place the materials in the center of the circle and follow the procedure described above. Encourage the children to think of all the possible combinations.

Happy or Sad?

Cut enough circles from construction paper to give one to each child. On one side of each circle, draw a happy face; on the other side draw a sad face (see the illustration). When the children are in the circle, give each a happy/sad face circle and have them practice showing the two sides by saying, "Show me the happy face; show me the sad face." Then give them the following situations and, after each one, ask if it would make them happy or sad. Have them show you their response with the appropriate side of the circle.

1. You lost your balloon.
2. You are going to the park to play.
3. You have to go to bed early.
4. You are going to have ice cream.
5. Your mom bought you new shoes.
6. You fell down and hurt your knee.

Variation: Allow older children to think of happy and sad situations for the group to respond to.

Shapes

Cut out a number of circles, squares, and triangles from construction paper. Pass one shape to each child seated in the circle. Check with the children to be sure that they know which shape they're holding. Then ask each child to find something in the room that is the same shape as his or her construction paper shape; have the children bring the objects to the circle. Call on the children to show their paper shapes and to share their objects with the others. Tell the children to exchange paper shapes and have them find new objects with the same shape.

34

One-on-One: Parent-Child Discrimination Activities

WHAT'S MISSING?

Collect some small toys, such as toy cars, plastic figures, or small blocks. Put three of the items on a tray. Show the tray to your child and ask him or her to look carefully at the items. Then take the tray out of your child's view and remove one of the items. Show your child the tray again and ask, "What's missing?" Allow your child to look at the items still on the tray and decide what is missing. Show the missing item and then play again using different toys.

LEAF COLLECTING

Take your child outside for a walk. Take a sack or bag with you and collect some leaves. Encourage your child to choose leaves that are in good shape and different from each other. Once inside, spread the leaves out on waxed paper. Examine the leaves carefully to see if you have any duplicates. Discuss the leaves' differences and likenesses. Then help your child glue each leaf onto a cardboard square with a small amount of white glue. Let the leaves dry. Take the leaves outside again and see if you and your child can match the leaves to the trees they came from. You may also want to look for other leaves that match those you glued to cardboard.

COLOR DISCRIMINATION

Cut color pictures of different foods from an old magazine and glue each picture onto an index card or heavy paper. Give the stack of picture cards to your child and assist him or her in sorting the foods into color groups. Then look for other groupings your child may be able to sort the pictures into: foods you eat for breakfast, meats, vegetables, fruits, breads and cereals, and so on.

CHAPTER 4

PROBLEM SOLVING

Problem solving activities are important because:

• Every aspect of a child's day involves problem solving of some kind.

• The development of thinking skills is critical to successful advancement in formal schooling and later life.

• The activities will enable young children to make reasonable predictions about an event and then observe the outcome.

To promote success in problem solving activities:

• Make the activities as concrete as possible. Provide materials that the children can manipulate and, whenever possible, use actual materials that the children are familiar with.

• Allow the children to experiment without telling them too much and without trying to guide the process for them. This will encourage problem solving, even if the experiment fails, since the children are allowed to draw their own conclusions.

• Set up activities that encourage the children to use and develop all their senses. Some children have very limited opportunities to use their sense of smell or touch.

• Encourage the children to manipulate materials into sets to develop a basic concept of numbers before abstract numerals become involved. Problem solving encourages children to make sets equal in quantity or quality.

Open, Please

Pass a sealed bag of non-flake-type cereal or marshmallows around the circle. Encourage each child to look at the bag carefully. When everyone has had a chance, ask the children, "How can we get this bag open?" Encourage the children to think of all the possible ways without showing your preference for one or the other. Continue the discussion, and then have the children choose what they think is the best method for opening the bag. Have one child use that method to try to open the bag. Then lead a discussion about the ease or problems in opening the bag and guide the children to another choice, if necessary. Once the bag is open, ask, "How can we divide the cereal (or marshmallows) evenly among us?" Lead another discussion, allowing the children to choose a method for dividing and distributing the food.

Variation: For older children, appoint a banker to count the pieces of food in the bag. Have the whole class brainstorm ways to distribute the food and then let the children pick and use the method they think is best.

Even Up

Draw three circles on the chalkboard or on a piece of poster board. Give each child one, two, or three small round crackers. Then go back to each child and say, "How many more crackers do you need to have as many circles as I have on the board?" If a child is unsure, give him or her the correct number of crackers to even up.

Variation: After you have worked with the activity several times, or when all the children have demonstrated that they can make sets of three, follow the procedure above with four circles and later with five.

Take Apart, Put Together

Gather together the following items: staple remover, tape, stapler, scissors, glue, hole punch, brads, hammer, yarn, paper clips, string, masking tape, rubber bands, screwdriver, and clothespins. Mark two shoe boxes as shown in the illustration. Put the boxes and all the items in the center of the circle. Ask a child to choose one item and tell the other children what the tool is and how it is used. Then ask the children, "Would this go in a box of tools that take things apart or in a box of tools that put things together?" Continue having the children sort all the tools into the appropriate boxes. Add the boxes to your art or construction center for children to use on various projects.

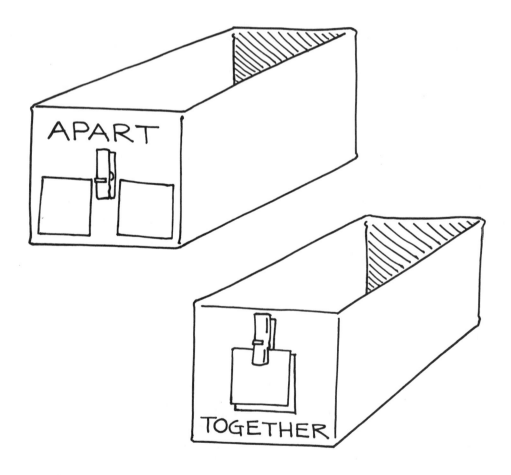

Graphing Favorites

Children can use their problem solving skills when they pick a favorite from a number of choices and when they're asked to predict what they think other children like. Make a graph and laminate it or cover it with clear Contact paper (see the illustration). Then decide on two foods you think most of the children like to eat, for example, pizza and hamburgers. Cut out magazine pictures of the foods and paper clip them to the top of the chart. Discuss the food choices with the children and ask, "Do you think most children like pizza or hamburgers best?" Allow some discussion and then have each child show a preference by placing a peel-off dot under the chosen picture. When everyone has made a choice, point to the chart and ask, "Can you look at the dots and tell which food our class likes best?"

Variations: Follow the same procedure choosing between two favorite colors, hot or cold weather, two types of outdoor play equipment, or pets. Children who can write their name can print it on a stick-on note and press the note on the graph.

39

Melting Snowballs

Use this activity after a significant snowfall or try it with ice cubes during warm weather. Have each child make a snowball and put it in a plastic sandwich bag. Write the child's name on a strip of masking tape and place it on the outside of the bag. Freeze all the bags until you are ready to do the activity. On a day when the sun is shining, lead a circle time discussion about what happens when the sun shines and the temperature warms up. Distribute the bags to their owners. Then take the children outside. Ask the children to predict what will happen to their snowballs if they are left outside in the sun. Encourage the children to make predictions about which snowball will melt first and which will last the longest. Place the snowballs, still in their bags, on a sidewalk or other nearby open area. Let the children check the bags frequently so that they see the results.

More or Less?

Make a spinner like the one in the illustration by cutting a circle from poster board or oak tag, adding the words and drawings, and attaching an arrow with a brad. Choose one child to hold the spinner. Before the child spins, say, "I'm thinking of three buttons." Signal the child to spin the arrow and announce the position it lands on. If the arrow is pointing to the "More" side, any child with more than three buttons on his or her clothes should stand. If the arrow is pointing to the "Less" side, any child with less than three buttons should stand. Pass the spinner to another child and use a different "I'm thinking of..." sentence. You might try:

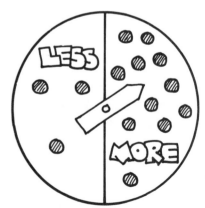

"I'm thinking of two ponytails."
"I'm thinking of one color on socks."
"I'm thinking of two colors on shirts."

Can You Tell a Story?

Choose a book that the children have not seen or had read to them. Bring the book to the circle and pass it around so each child can see the cover. Ask the children what they think the book is about. Record each child's answer on chart paper beside the child's name. Then read the book aloud to the children. Afterward, check the chart paper and review the prediction each child made. Ask the children if the prediction is close to what the story was about. If it is, put a star by the child's name. At another circle time, remind the children of the story by reviewing the chart. Read the predictions with a star beside them. Then read the story again.

Mystery Box

Wrap a familiar small stuffed animal or doll in a box with tissue paper. Seal the box with masking tape. Bring the box to circle time and set in on the floor in front of your chair. Wait until one of the children asks what is in the box. Ask the child what he or she thinks could be in it. Pass the box around the circle and allow the children to shake the box to see if it makes any sounds. If necessary, give the children some clues about the animal or doll in the box. For example, you could say, "This box has something in it that you would like to rest with at nap time" or "This box is holding a friend of ours from the housekeeping area." If no one guesses what's in the box, put it where the children can see it and suggest that they think some more about what might be in the box. At the next circle time, ask again what the children think is in the box. Continue giving hints about the contents until one of the children figures it out.

Guess My Special Prize

You can use this game to encourage children to come to the circle and use their thinking skills. Before circle time begins, ask one child to help you find a special prize to keep as a secret from the other children. Find something the child can hide in a pocket or in his or her hand. When the children are gathered in the circle, announce, "Andrea has a special prize. She is going to give you a clue and your job is to see if you can guess what the prize is." After the clue is given, allow the children to guess the prize. Provide more hints if necessary. Let the child who guesses the prize keep it.

Shapes

Use a marker to draw a circle on a piece of chart paper. Ask the children to help you think what the circle could become if you added more lines to it. Children might suggest, for example, a soccer ball, a balloon, or a beach ball. Make a list of the answers you get below the circle. When the list is complete, review the possibilities aloud and choose a child to pick one he or she would like to see the circle become. Have that child choose another child to make the circle into the chosen drawing. Repeat the procedure using a square, a triangle, and an oval.

1. SOCCER BALL 4. MOON
2. BALLOON   5.
3. BEACH BALL   6.

Green Cheese

Bring a container of cottage cheese and some green food coloring to the circle. Allow one child to put the cottage cheese into a large bowl. Hand out a plastic spoon to each child. Then pass the cottage cheese around the circle and allow those who want to to taste it. Ask the children what the cottage cheese would taste like if it were green. Encourage all answers. Pour a small amount of the food coloring into the cottage cheese and choose one child to stir it until the cottage cheese turns green. Pass the bowl around the circle again and, after each child has had a taste, ask if the color makes the cottage cheese taste any different. Determine how many children think the change of color makes the food taste different and how many think it tastes the same. Graph the results.

Variation: Let older children follow the procedure above and then ask them what new color they would like to add to the green cottage cheese. Ask them what color the cottage cheese would turn. Allow the children to add the color and see what new color they make.

What Do They Open?

Use the collection box of keys from the activity "Class Collections" in Chapter 3. Discuss the keys and what they might open. Pass the box around the circle and ask each child to take one key out of the box. When every child has a key, ask what the key opens. Encourage the children to elaborate on their answers. For example, if a child says his key opens a door, ask him which door, in what house, who is in the house, or why the door is locked.

43

One-on-One: Parent-Child Problem Solving Activities

WHAT'S THE ANSWER?

Look for opportunities to let your child figure out the solution to a problem on his or her own. For example, you might allow your child to suggest a way to open a sealed food product; decide how many plates and utensils are required for a family meal; or determine how to evenly divide snacks at playtime.

THE TOOLBOX

Let your child explore your family toolbox or a drawer of kitchen gadgets. Encourage your child to guess what function the various tools have. Be sure to let your child handle only those tools that are safe. Brainstorming a good number of possible functions for each tool will help your child develop strong problem solving skills.

PLANNING A MEAL

Allow your child to help with meal planning. For example, if you say that you have planned chicken for dinner, your child can help you decide how the chicken should be prepared and what other foods should go with it. Encourage your child to think about what other family members like and don't like to eat, the colors of the different foods being prepared, and which foods are available.

EVEN UP

Use small snack crackers to play the game Even Up. Give two crackers to your child and take three for yourself. Ask your child if you both have the same number of crackers and, if you don't, how many more your child needs to have the same. Allow your child to take a cracker to make the number of crackers even. Then, eat one cracker and ask your child again if you both have the same number of crackers. Play Even Up with other things.

CHAPTER 5
PATTERNING

Patterning activities are important because:
• They can organize young children's observations about the things around them.
• Patterning skills are necessary for beginning reading and math concepts.
• When children are introduced to the concept of patterning, they will begin to look for patterns in the many things they do throughout each day.

To promote success in patterning activities:
• Encourage children to make observations and to look for patterns in everyday materials. Children can organize even the most simple materials into a simple pattern, such as A/B/A.
• Use circle time to demonstrate to the children how they can create their own patterns and to evaluate their readiness to find patterns in their work.
• Teach the children to say a pattern out loud once one has been created. At circle time you can ask two children to work together on a pattern, perhaps red crayons, blue crayons, red crayons. Then ask another child or group of children to point to the pattern and say it: red, blue, red.

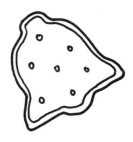

Vegetable Patterns

Collect several each of two different-colored raw vegetables, perhaps carrots and green beans or cucumbers and potatoes. Place the vegetables in the center of the circle and lead a short discussion about them, including their names and how they taste. Then ask two children to put the vegetables in a row stretching across the circle. Watch how the children make the row, either by putting all of one kind of vegetable together or in a random way. Ask if any of the children can see a way of placing the vegetables so that they go bean, carrot, bean, carrot. Allow two children to make the adjustments. Then ask another child to point to each vegetable as you say the pattern as a group. Put the vegetables in an area where the children can work with them later independently.

Variation: Let older children work with three different vegetables.

People Patterns

Divide the children into two groups: those with dark hair and those with light hair. Ask one child to place the children in a pattern of one light-haired child followed by one dark-haired child. When all the children are in place, begin with the child sitting to your left and have each say if he or she represents dark hair or light hair in the pattern. When everyone has spoken, ask the children to say the pattern aloud as a group.

Variations: Let the children make patterns using other characteristics or clothing: colors of shirts, tie or slip-on shoes, or, for older children, eye color.

Cars and Blocks

Fill a basket with toy cars and another with wooden or plastic blocks. Place the baskets on the floor in front of you in the circle. Review any patterning activities you have done with the children. Then pass around the two baskets and ask the children to take two items from each basket. When all the children have four items, instruct them to choose a partner and combine their toys to make a pattern. Encourage working together as you move around the circle to see what patterns the children have made. Some pairs may be able to make a second pattern with their same materials. After the children have had time to work, share the patterns with the whole group.

Unit Block Patterns

To encourage the children to look for patterns without reference to color, use wooden unit blocks. Bring several each of two different block shapes to the circle. Ask two children to work together to make a pattern with the blocks. You may need to encourage them to look for ways to make patterns using the shapes of the blocks or help them to place the blocks. Ask the children to help you say the pattern out loud when it's completed. Continue to choose pairs of children to look for new patterns using the same blocks.

Variation: Older children may use three different block shapes to make more complicated patterns.

Color Dots

Glue a piece of chart paper to poster board or mount it on a low bulletin board. Cut apart one sheet each of two different colors of peel-off dots so that each dot is separate. Put all the dots in one basket and ask each child in the circle to take two dots out without looking. When all the children have their dots, go around the circle and have each child say what color dots he or she has: two red, two yellow, or a red and a yellow. Then ask one child to peel off the backing of one of the dots and stick the dot on the far left side of the chart paper. Allow the child to choose another child and, if he or she has a different-colored dot, press it on the paper next to the first dot. If the second child doesn't have a different-colored dot, another child should be chosen. Continue having the children add dots in an alternating color pattern until all the dots have been used or there are no more of the necessary color.

Variation: Older children may work with three different colors of dots.

Cookie Break

At snack time, bring two different kinds of cookies to the circle. Ask several children to hand out the cookies by alternating the kind they give to each student. Encourage the children to say the name of each cookie as it's being given out. Ask the children who are distributing cookies to stop at various points in the circle and have the next child predict what kind of cookie he or she will receive. At other snack times you might distribute different kinds of crackers, fruit, or colored napkins.

Pattern Sounds

Cut enough small squares out of red, blue, and yellow construction paper to keep one of each color for yourself and to give one of any color to each of the children. Ask the children to help you designate a sound for each color; red could be a finger snap, blue might be a clap, and yellow might be a foot tap. Have everyone practice making the sounds several times by holding up the color squares. Then tell the children to watch carefully as you hold up a color square. Have the children who have the same color square make the appropriate sound. Hold the squares up in a predictable pattern. Start with an easy one, for example, red, blue, yellow. Later on, have the children pass their card to the child next to them, and hold up the cards in a new pattern.

Variation: Let older children try a more complicated pattern, for example, red, red, yellow, blue.

In the Circle

Ask the children to create a pattern in the circle by sitting in a certain way, for example, folded legs, legs outstretched, and so on. Have the children look at everyone in the circle and say the pattern. Then ask each child to think of another way to sit and change the pattern. Make a high-low pattern by having some of the children lean down and some stand up. Make the activity more gamelike by asking the first child on your left to think of a certain way to sit and then to get into that position. Ask the child to the left of the first child to sit differently. Encourage the rest of the children to mimic the first or second child in the circle, creating a new pattern.

Macaroni Necklaces

Bring to class a good amount of three different dried pastas, such as elbow macaroni, pinwheels, and tube-shaped pasta, for the children to string into necklaces. Let the children help you dye the pasta with different colors of food coloring. Place each type of pasta in a large plastic container that has a lid and add a small amount of rubbing alcohol and some food coloring; the more food coloring you add, the brighter the color will be. Leave the pasta at least one hour, or until the color intensity is what you like. Remove the pasta with a strainer and let the pieces dry on newspaper overnight.

Cut lengths of yarn for the necklaces. Dip one end of each yarn length in white glue and allow it to dry. At circle time, let each child choose any two colors of pasta (let older children choose three) to string onto the yarn in a pattern. Have the children lay their pasta out in front of them for you to check their pattern before stringing. Tie the necklaces on the children and go around the circle allowing each child to say his or her pattern. You may wish to keep some colored pasta in bowls on a shelf for children to make patterns individually at another time.

Variation: Help the children discover that they can make patterns with different colors of the same kind of pasta, or by alternating turned-up pieces of elbow macaroni with pieces turned down.

50

Bean Patterns

Paint one side of a good number of large uncooked beans with white tempera paint. Allow the beans to dry thoroughly on waxed paper. At circle time, provide each child with a handful of beans. Allow the children time to play with the beans on the floor in front of them. Then ask the children to look for a pattern in the way the beans are laying. Some children will discover that by turning some beans over and moving others around they can create a pattern. Continue to encourage the children to experiment with their beans to see how many patterns they can make.

Mosaic Tiles

Bring a number of tile samples to the circle (a flooring store may give you some discontinued pieces). Allow the children to play with the materials for a time. Then ask them to work together to tile the inside of the circle. Observe the patterns that emerge and point them out to the children. Store the tiles in a box in your manipulatives or building area for the children to use at individual activity time.

Saying Patterns

Give each pair of students a strip of art paper and two or three different styles of familiar stickers. Ask each pair to place their stickers on the paper strip in a pattern. Move around the circle and assist the children if they need help. Ask each pair if they know what to call each of their stickers. When the patterns are complete, use a marker to put an asterisk on the left side of each paper strip. Then ask the children to exchange papers with another pair of children. Allow the children to say the pattern they receive, starting from the asterisk. Encourage any two children who would like to read their pattern to the group. Display the patterns on a low bulletin board.

Collections

Put several of the collection boxes from the activity "Class Collections" in Chapter 3 in the center of the circle. Give each child a blank sheet of white typing or art paper. Instruct the children to choose two things from each box to work with. When all the children have chosen their items, encourage them to lay the materials on their paper and make a pattern. Move around the circle to see the different kinds of patterns the children make. Encourage them to create as many different patterns as they can.

Variation: Older children may use white glue to permanently mount their patterns on heavy paper or cardboard.

Rhythms

Demonstrate to the children how to make clapping patterns. Clap a simple pattern such as two short claps, pause, one clap. Ask the children to repeat the pattern. Then clap it again and have the children repeat it once more. Change the pattern, perhaps to one clap, pause, one clap, pause, two short claps. Have the children repeat the pattern several times. Over the next several days, make the patterns more difficult. Also allow the children to think of patterns for the group to follow.

Variations: If most of the children can snap their fingers, you can include snaps in the pattern: one clap, two snaps, one clap, and so on. You can also play a game with older children by making up a pattern and calling on a child to repeat it. If the child repeats it correctly, he or she can make up a pattern and call on another child to repeat it.

In and Out

Place the children's chairs in a circle, all facing in. Ask the children to choose a chair to sit in. Pick one child and assist him or her in turning the chair to face out. Emphasize to the children that Ashley is sitting facing out of the circle. Ask a child two children away from the first child to turn his or her chair facing out. Continue choosing every other child in the circle to sit facing out. When every other child is facing out, help the children move the chairs to face in again. Then ask the child to your left to face his or her chair out. Ask the next child to continue the in-out pattern—should the chair face in or out? Ask each child which way the chair should face to complete the pattern.

One-on-One: Parent-Child Patterning Activities

VEGETABLE PATTERNS

Put out several each of two different-colored raw vegetables, perhaps carrots and cucumbers. Ask your child to put the vegetables in a row, one after the other, to make a pattern. Say the pattern as you point to each vegetable. Then have your child look for other patterns to make: two carrots, one cucumber, two carrots, one cucumber, and so on.

TOY CARS

Gather a number of toy cars to help your child create patterns. Encourage your child to put the cars in a row to show a pattern. Say the pattern as you point to each car. Experiment with several different patterns using the cars, for example, a pattern that uses the colors of cars, the kinds of cars, or the size of cars.

SNACK TIME PATTERNS

Put some squares of cheese and some snack crackers on a large plate. Encourage your child to make different patterns with the food. For example, he or she might put a cheese square on top of each cracker, or make a pattern of cheese square, cracker, cheese square, cracker.

PATTERN SOUNDS

Clap your hands in a pattern and encourage your child to repeat the pattern. Try the pattern of two short claps, one clap, two short claps, one clap. After your child repeats it several times, make a more difficult pattern or include finger snaps if your child can do them.

CHAPTER 6

MUSIC

Music activities are important because:

• They help to get and keep children's attention in a positive way.

• They are excellent for developing children's short-term memory.

• Most any skill that is appropriate for young children to learn can be taught through music activities.

• Parents often learn about their child's activities in school by listening to the songs the child repeats at home.

• Involvement in music activities can help all children feel successful.

To promote success in music activities:

• Use the many excellent recordings for children that are available if you are avoiding music activities because you don't have a trained voice or play a musical instrument. Many of the songs provided in this chapter are based on familiar songs you can sing without musical accompaniment.

• Provide music activities during circle time as a way to relax or wind down after more physical activity or to bring the group together after they have been working independently. Music helps children focus their energy in a new direction.

• Let the children have fun making up songs. When you demonstrate that a song can be used for most any situation, you will find that the children begin to create their own songs.

• Use the same song for the same activity each day, for example, when preparing for snack time. Many of the songs in this chapter give children a structure for following directions, and when you use them consistently they will help children be able to anticipate what is expected.

The Good Morning Song

This song can signal to the children that they should gather in the circle to get ready for the start of the day.

Good morning, good morning,
Good morning, how are you?
I'm fine, I'm fine,
I hope that you are too.

Hello, My Friends, and How Are You?

This song welcomes the children to the classroom at the beginning of the day. It may also be used when children return from being away, or on other occasions when you want to sing as a group or sing to small groups or one child.

Hello, my friends, and how are you?
Hello, my friends, I missed you too.
Sit down now and let's begin.

56

Getting Ready for Fun

This song is a good one to sing when you want to get the children set for a new activity or are anticipating giving them game directions. Sing it to the tune of "The Hokey Pokey."

First you put your hands right in your lap,
Then you watch my eyes with your eyes with all your might.
When we all are ready we'll begin to do,
Something fun
That you will like
And I'll like too!

Are You Listening?

This is another good song for preparing the children for a listening activity or to help them get ready to receive directions. Use the name of a child who is demonstrating to you that he or she is ready to listen. Sing to the tune of "Are You Sleeping?" ("Frère Jacques").

Are you listening, are you listening?
Hear our song, hear our song.
Dana, are you ready? Kyle, are you ready?
Listening song, listening song.

If you need or want to sing more verses, ask the child whose name you called to choose another child and put that name in the song. You may also add motions like the following:

Cup your hands behind your ears.
Hold hands outstretched.
Point to the child whose name is used in the song.
Cup your hands behind your ears.

Be a Friend Today

This song is a positive way to start the day and to encourage the children to think of things they can do for others. After singing the song once, stop and ask the children to think of something they can do to show someone they are a friend. Then sing the song again and ask if anyone thought of a way to be a friend. Allow the child to respond and then sing the song again. Sing to the tune of "Jingle Bells."

Be a friend, be a friend,
Be a friend today.
Tell me one thing you can do
To be a friend today.

The Emotions Song

Use the various verses of this song to help children discuss their feelings. Sing to the tune of "If You're Happy and You Know It."

If you're happy and you know it, show a smile.
If you're happy and you know it, show a smile.
If you're happy and you know it, then your smile
  will surely show it.
If you're happy and you know it, show a smile.
If you're sad and you know it, show a frown.
If you're sad and you know it, show a frown.
If you're sad and you know it, then your frown
  will surely show it.
If you're sad and you know it, show a frown.

Variations: You may want to make additional verses for lonely, mad, excited, and scared.

58

Christy's Here Today

This song will help a child who arrives late for class feel welcome and a part of the activities. Insert the child's name and sing to the tune of "The Farmer in the Dell."

Christy's here today.
Christy's here today.
Come and join your friends at school.
Christy's here today.

The After Work-Time Song

Use this song to begin a discussion after the children have completed an individual activity period. Insert the child's name and sing to the tune of "Twinkle, Twinkle, Little Star."

Kathy, Kathy, can you say
What you did in your work today?

Allow the child whose name was used in the song to tell something about his or her activity. Then sing the song again using another child's name.

The Sun Is Out Today

This music activity will help children focus on the weather. Ask one child to report the weather to the group. Then, depending on what the weather conditions are, sing one of the following verses to the tune of "The Farmer in the Dell."

The sun is out today.
The sun is out today.
Oh, my, how warm it feels.
The sun is out today.

It's rainy out today.
It's rainy out today.
Oh, my, how wet I get.
It's rainy out today.

It's cold outside today.
It's cold outside today.
Oh, my, how chilly I feel.
It's cold outside today.

What Will You Be for Halloween?

Sing this song enough times for each of the children to respond to the question "What will you be for Halloween?" Pause after each verse and encourage the child whose name is in the song to tell about his or her costume. Then begin again using a different child's name. Sing to the tune of "Mary Had a Little Lamb."

What will you be for Halloween? Halloween? Halloween?
What will you be for Halloween? Ricky, tell us please.

Variation: Let older children print their names on chart paper and point in order to each name on the list so that the group will know whose name will be sung next. After each child talks about what he or she will be, write the costume down beside the name.

The Shape Song

Cut out a number of circles, squares, and triangles from construction paper. Keep one of each shape for yourself and distribute one shape to each child in the circle. Then sing "The Shape Song" with the group and hold up each shape as it is named. Encourage the children to hold up the appropriate shapes too. After singing the song through, have the children exchange shapes and sing the song again. Sing to the tune of "The Mulberry Bush."

When we know the shapes in our world,
We always like to show you.
If you have a square in your hand,
Let me see you know it.

The Color Game

Begin this singing game by cutting out a number of squares of familiar colors of construction paper. Pass out a square to each child. Choose one child to be the leader. Start the singing and instruct the leader to walk around the inside of the circle. When the singing stops after the last line of the song, have the leader point to the child nearest him or her in the circle. That child says the name of the color square he or she is holding. If the child is correct, have him or her join the leader and, holding hands, walk around the circle. Sing the song again, continuing until all the children have named their color and are holding hands. Sing to the tune of "Row, Row, Row Your Boat."

Colors, colors, colors will come,
Singing loud and true.
When the colors hear their name,
They will stand with you.

Getting Ready for Snack Time

This song tells the children how to prepare for snack time. Sing to the tune of "Are You Sleeping?" ("Frère Jacques").

Wash your hands, wash your hands.
Time for snacks, time for snacks.
Use the soap and water, use the soap and water.
Come right back, come right back.

Variation: You may want to add the following twist to have the children prepare in smaller groups:

Girls wash your hands, girls wash your hands, or
Boys wash your hands, boys wash your hands.

Let's Clean the Classroom Now

Let this spin-off song help you assign certain children to straighten up various areas after a play period or before leaving for the day. Sing the first verse while the children are sitting in the circle. Then, as you begin the second verse, move around the circle pointing to several children to clean up the areas being named in the song. Sing to the tune of "Do You Know the Muffin Man?"

Let us clean the classroom now,
The classroom now, the classroom now.
Let us clean the classroom now, singing as we go.

You clean the doll house (art corner, etc.) now,
The doll house now, the doll house now.
You clean the doll house now, singing as we go.

The Good-Bye Song

To let the children know that the end of the school day has arrived, sing this song followed by "The Dismissal Song" below. Sing this song to the tune of "London Bridge."

Now it's time to say good-bye, say good-bye, say good-bye.
Now it's time to say good-bye,
See you in the morning.

Have the children wave their hands as they sing. If your class doesn't meet every day, substitute the next meeting day in the last line of the song.

The Dismissal Song

You can use this song to dismiss small groups of children at a time. Sing to the tune of "Good Night, Ladies."

Good-bye, Patrick,
Good-bye, Jeannie,
Good-bye, Morgan,
We'll see you all again.

Continue singing the verse, adding three new names each time, until all the children have been dismissed for the day.

Variation: Use the song to send small groups of children to other activities by changing the last line:

You may go to lunch, or
You may go to rest, or
You may go to play.

One-on-One: Parent-Child Music Activities

BE A FRIEND TODAY
You can use this song to encourage your child to be a good friend. Sing it to the tune of "Jingle Bells."

Be a friend, be a friend,
Be a friend today.
Tell me one thing you can do
To be a friend today.

THE EMOTIONS SONG
Sing this song to help your child discuss how he or she is feeling. Sing to the tune of "If You're Happy and You Know It."

If you're happy and you know it, show a smile.
If you're happy and you know it, show a smile.
If you're happy and you know it, then your smile will surely
    show it.
If you're happy and you know it, show a smile.

Try singing other verses about being sad, lonely, mad, excited, or scared.

THE AFTER SCHOOL SONG
Try singing this song to start your child telling you about his or her school day. Insert your child's name and sing to the tune of "Twinkle, Twinkle, Little Star."

Kathy, Kathy, can you say
What you did at school today?

THE SUN IS OUT TODAY
This song can lead to a discussion of the day's weather. Sing to the tune of "The Farmer in the Dell."

The sun is out today.
The sun is out today.
Oh, my, how warm it feels.
The sun is out today.

Use other verses when appropriate, such as, "It's cold out today," "It's rainy out today," or "There are clouds today."